MAGELLAN
VOYAGER WITH A DREAM

FERDINAN:MAGAGLIANES

MAGELLAN
VOYAGER WITH A DREAM

by William Jay Jacobs

Franklin Watts
New York / Chicago / London / Toronto / Sydney
A First Book

Cover illustration by Amy Wasserman
Cover photographs copyright ©: North Wind Picture Archives, Alfred, Me. (map and
ships); Stock Montage/Historical Pictures Service, Chicago, Il. (portrait and astrolabe).

Photographs copyright ©: Art Resource, NY: pp. 2 (Scala), 15 (Giraudon), 26 (Alinari),
28 (Erich Lessing); Archive Photos, NYC: p. 12; Robert Frerck/Odyssey/Chicago: p. 13;
North Wind Picture Archives: pp. 17, 19, 24, 31, 36, 37, 40, 45, 47, 54; Stock
Montage/Historical Pictures Service: pp. 22, 41, 50, 51; The Bettmann Archive: pp. 33,
56; Photo Researchers Inc./ Mary Evans Picture Library: p. 43.

Library of Congress Cataloging-in-Publication Data
Jacobs, William Jay
Magellan: voyager with a dream / by William Jay Jacobs
p. cm. — (A First Book)
Includes bibliographical references and index.
ISBN 0-531-20139-2
1. Magalhães, Fernão de, d. 1521 — Juvenile literature.
2. Explorers—Portugal—Biography—Juvenile literature.
3. Voyages around the world — Juvenile literature. (1. Magellan, Ferdinand, d. 1521.
2. Explorers. 3. Voyages around the world.] I. Title. II. Series.
G420.M2J33 1994
910'.92—dc20   93-29698
[B]   CIP AC

CONTENTS

FOREWORD
9

CHAPTER ONE
YOUTH AND EARLY VOYAGES
11

CHAPTER TWO
A DARING PLAN
21

CHAPTER THREE
MUTINY!
30

CHAPTER FOUR
TRIUMPH
39

CHAPTER FIVE
TRAGEDY
49

AFTERMATH
53

IMPORTANT DATES
58

FOR FURTHER READING
59

INDEX
61

He gained a world; he gave that world
Its grandest lesson: "On! Sail on!"
— JOAQUIN CINCINNATUS MILLER

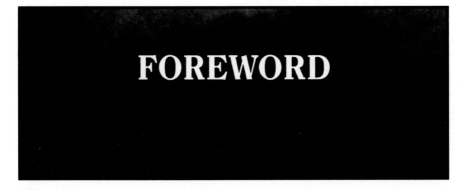

FOREWORD

Today we know our planet well. We know its continents and its oceans. We have fine maps to help us find our way when we travel. But it was not always that way. Once, long ago, there was a boy named Ferdinand Magellan, who wondered about the world. "How big is it?" he must have asked. "Is it really round, as some people are saying? And if it really is round, could we get to places in the east by sailing to the west? Is there a way for ships to sail through the strange new world that Christopher Columbus came upon?"

In the years after Columbus's fateful voyage of discovery, such questions also filled the minds of rulers in the countries of western Europe, especially the leaders of Portugal, Spain, England and Holland. Which country, they wondered, will gain the best route to the fabulous riches of India and China and the "Spice Islands" near the Straits of Malacca? And who will eventually come to own those riches — all the spices, the jewelry, the gold and silver? To people living in Europe, this new wealth was far beyond anything they had ever believed possible.

9

Magellan's youth came at a time in history when young people joined with their national leaders in dreaming of the fame and riches they might gain someday by sailing to the newly discovered lands. Fortune and everlasting glory could be theirs, as well as a chance to convert the native peoples they met to the religion of Europe, Christianity.

Thus, beginning in the late 1400s, "Gospel, Glory, and Gold," along with the sheer joy of adventure, became the burning ambitions of many people, both young and old. They were goals that would last for more than two centuries in what would become known as The Age of Discovery.

It was one of history's most exciting times. And of all the great explorers who roamed the seas in that storied time, none contributed more to human knowledge than Ferdinand Magellan. He commanded the voyage that was the first to circumnavigate the globe — to sail completely around the planet — proving that the world is, indeed, really round.

The story of Magellan is one of great struggle and suffering, of plots against the explorer's life, and of wounds received in bloody battles on distant fields of combat. Yet, from Magellan's story there is much we all can learn about the dreams of adventurers that, for so many centuries, have helped to shape the course of human society.

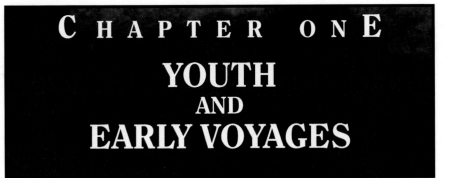

CHAPTER ONE

YOUTH
AND
EARLY VOYAGES

Ferdinand Magellan probably was born in Operto, Portugal, in the year 1480, twelve years before Columbus landed in the Americas. Although not wealthy, the Magellan family belonged to the Portuguese nobility. Young Ferdinand had an older sister, Isobel, and an older brother, Diogo. Together, the children would picnic and play games on the grounds of their pleasant family estate. They attended church services and feasts. And often, along with tenants on the estate, they danced by torchlight well into the night.

In school, Ferdinand and his brother learned to ride horses. They learned how to handle swords, both right handed and left handed in case of injury. But most important, they studied mapmaking and how to use the stars to find their way while sailing on the seas. Portugal at that time was a nation that lived the life of the sea. Its traders and explorers traveled everywhere. And to most young Portuguese boys there were no greater heroes than the naval heroes.

*Operto, Portugal, the probable
birthplace of Magellan*

 12

It was in 1443 that Portugal's Prince Henrique, known as "Prince Henry the Navigator," had built a castle at Sagres that jutted out on a rocky point of land into the sea. There he gathered experts in geography, astronomy, navigation, and ship construction. Inspired by Prince Henry, Portuguese seamen began to sail farther and farther south along the western coast of Africa. In 1487, Bartholomew Diaz rounded the southern tip of Africa, the Cape of Good Hope.

In 1498, Vasco da Gama sailed around the Cape and arrived in Calicut, India. Da Gama eventually returned

Prince Henry the Navigator built his famous school of navigation on top of the seacoast cliff at Sagres.

to Portugal with a fortune in spices, silks, emeralds, and pearls. In 1502, da Gama led a fleet of ten ships to Calicut and Cochin on the Malabar coast of India. As a result of those voyages, the once-legendary wealth of Cathay (China) and of Cipangu (Japan) soon became real to the people of Europe. Almost overnight, Portugal was recognized, along with Spain, as one of the two leading powers in the Western world.

Exciting events such as those shaped the youth and early adulthood of Ferdinand Magellan. In 1492, when Ferdinand was twelve years old, he left the family estate to join his brother as a page in the household of Leonora, the queen of Portugal. Only a few months later, in March 1493, Christopher Columbus touched the coast of Portugal on his return to Spain from the great voyage that marked Europe's first significant encounter with the New World.

Could it really be, Europeans buzzed, that Columbus was right, that a ship could reach India, in the east, by sailing to the west? Like so many of his friends, Magellan eagerly looked forward to the time when he, too — like Diaz, da Gama, and Columbus — could sail the seas, returning home to wildly cheering crowds and, perhaps, to great wealth.

While young Ferdinand was a page to the queen, his father died. Then his mother died. But Magellan, tough-minded and ambitious for success, refused to become discouraged. Instead, he worked hard to win a place

Vasco da Gama

15

with the Portuguese forces then building fortresses and thriving trading posts in places as far away as Singapore and Canton, a distance of some 6,000 miles (9,600 km).

In 1505, Magellan finally got his chance. He was accepted as a crew member by a fleet of twenty-two ships with 1,500 soldiers led by the Portuguese viceroy of India, Francisco de Almeida. The mission of the fleet was to gain control for Portugal of the sea-lanes from the Red Sea and the eastern coast of Africa all the way across the Indian Ocean to Goa on the western coast of India.

Muslims (or "Moors") had held a monopoly on these trade routes. Goods from the profitable trade with Asia were usually taken to the port of Alexandria, Egypt. From there merchants from the Italian city of Venice would sell them for high prices to eager buyers all across Europe.

Now the Portuguese fleet changed all that. In one bloody battle, Almeida and his soldiers captured the Arab stronghold of Mombasa, a key port city on the eastern coast of Africa. Other land and sea battles followed, with the Portuguese winning again and again. Finally, Portugal came to control the territory of Goa in India. There they built a center for trade and commerce with Asia.

Ferdinand Magellan had eagerly thrown himself into the fighting. By the end of his first year of service with Almeida, he was in charge of a small ship with six

16

cannons. By fiercely attacking the poorly equipped Moors, he was able to sink more than two hundred of their vessels. When the Portuguese fleet landed on the Malabar coast of India, Magellan again distinguished himself in battle. In one skirmish, he was seriously wounded, but he recovered. From Cochin, India, he sailed to Singapore and Malacca, the busy commercial

The market in Goa, India, was controlled by the Portuguese.

ports commanding the Straits of Malacca, which links the Indian Ocean and the South China Sea, and is the gateway to China, Japan, and the fabled Spice Islands to the east.

It was at Malacca that Magellan first distinguished himself as a hero. There, in the crowded harbor, were gathered many ships from China, Burma, Malaya, and a variety of Moorish powers. The Portuguese commanders looked forward to filling the holds of their own vessels with rich cargoes of ginger, cloves, cinnamon, and pepper.

But little did the Europeans know that Sultan Mohammed of Malacca had gathered a force of soldiers to surprise them. By killing them all, the sultan hoped to discourage Portugal from extending its power beyond India and eventually into the Spice Islands to the east.

One night, Magellan was left to guard the Portuguese vessels while his commander, Francisco Serrano, and many of the soldiers went ashore for pleasure. Suddenly, Magellan saw the advancing Malayan forces. Without hesitation, he launched a boat filled with Portuguese troops toward the shore. Surviving a storm of lances and arrows, he and his men managed to rescue from the assault most of their comrades, including Serrano.

From that time on, Magellan was known as a soldier of great courage, boldness, and unbending will. He also was known as a leader who cared about the safety of

*Powerful warships helped
Portugal become a leading power.*

his men. As a reward for his heroism, he was given the rank of captain and put in command of a caravel, the most powerful of the Portuguese warships. It was at that time, too, that Magellan bought a Malayan slave, a

19

thirteen-year-old boy named Henrique, or "Black Henry," who was destined to remain with him for the rest of the explorer's life.

Returning to Portugal, Magellan was sent in 1513 to fight the Moors in Morocco. There, he was badly wounded in battle when an Arab lance pierced his leg. Close to death, he spent five months recuperating. He finally recovered, but for the rest of his life he walked with a severe limp. By the time of his lameness, Ferdinand Magellan was a man in his early thirties. Already he had lived a life of adventure and excitement, one that for most people would have been more than satisfying. Magellan, however, was far from satisfied. He had dreams of far greater enterprises, of far greater and more lasting fame.

CHAPTER TWO
A DARING PLAN

Because of the injury to his leg, Magellan was given an administrative job in Africa, one far removed from the scene of battle. He was placed in charge of the great storehouses containing loot seized from the Moors. That booty, along with the riches captured in the conquest of Goa, had made Portugal wealthier than any kingdom since imperial Rome in ancient times.

Magellan was a good manager. Yet, somehow, a number of animals he was responsible for were stolen. He was accused of stealing them himself and then selling them back to the Moors. Although ultimately cleared of all charges, he was embarrassed and angered by the accusations. Returning to Portugal, he personally presented himself before King Manuel I. The two men had never liked or trusted one another. Now, the crippled explorer knelt before the king. Humbly, he begged the monarch for at least some money in reward for his eight years of loyal service in places of great danger.

King Manuel I

With scorn, Manuel refused the request. Still on his knees, Magellan asked for command of a caravel so he could journey to India in hopes of earning the money he needed. Again the king refused.

22

Humiliated and angry, Magellan managed to hold his temper. Gently he asked whether the king would then allow him to serve overseas for another ruler. Waving his hand, King Manuel declared that he did not care what Ferdinand Magellan did or where he might go. The discussion, he announced, was over. Magellan finally asked for the honor of kissing the king's hand. But even that Manuel refused.

For many months afterward, Magellan thought of what had happened that day. Still embarrassed and bitter, he slowly began to form a plan that would restore his fortune, as well as his reputation. His plan was based on a secret map hidden in the treasury of the Portuguese king. As a member of a noble family serving in the royal court, Magellan once had seen the map, one prepared by a navigator who had sailed southward along the coast of Brazil.

Although the navigator had been forced out to sea by a storm, he returned to Portugal with an amazing suggestion. He claimed that there was a strait, a narrow passageway of water, through South America opening at the west to another vast ocean.

Magellan did not know that the map was wrong. The strait it showed was actually only a river, extending inland from the Atlantic Ocean into the interior of Brazil. But the map held out for him an important hope. It was the idea that by sailing west from Portugal, or perhaps from Spain, he could make his way through the New World and then by sea, reach the fabled Spice Islands.

If that ever happened, Magellan would become fabulously wealthy. The spices he then could ship to

A village in the Spanish-controlled Spice Islands

Europe were in enormous demand. They were used to flavor foods and to make perfumes. They were also used to improve the taste of beer and to help prepare corpses for burial. Pepper, cloves, nutmeg, cinnamon. Such ingredients made life more pleasant. And people were willing to pay for them. Magellan would be rich!

How to finance the trip? Clearly, King Manuel of Portugal would not support him in his search, but perhaps another monarch would. The one Magellan had in mind was the seventeen-year-old King Carlos I of Spain, best known to history as Emperor Charles V of the Holy Roman Empire.

In the autumn of 1517, limping as always, Magellan crossed the border into Spain, accompanied by his slave, Henrique. Soon he presented himself in Seville at the court of the king.

Immediately, young King Charles liked and trusted him. Charles already had heard much about the Portuguese adventurer's courage in battle. Now he was impressed with Magellan's great knowledge of navigation. Before long, the Spanish monarch also became fascinated by Magellan's stories of his experiences in the Indies. Most of all, Charles was tempted by the possibility of a Spanish-controlled route to the Spice Islands, a pathway that might compete with the Portuguese route to Asia around the tip of Africa, the Cape of Good Hope.

25

Young King Carlos I of Spain,
better known as Emperor Charles V

26

King Charles decided to take a chance. He ordered that funds be provided for an expedition "to discover unknown lands." And he appointed Ferdinand Magellan as captain-general of the expedition. The king was to provide the explorer with five ships and their crews, along with arms, ammunition, and supplies to last for two years. Magellan was to receive a small percentage of the profits from the journey itself as well as the right for himself and his heirs to govern all of the lands he discovered.

For a year and a half, Magellan carefully prepared for the voyage. He purchased five ships: the *Trinidad*, which was to be his flagship, the *Victoria*, the *San Antonio*, the *Concepción*, and the *Santiago*. He personally supervised the reconstruction of the vessels, strengthening them for the long voyage that lay ahead.

Recruiting crews for the ships proved difficult. Because Magellan refused to reveal the destination of his fleet, many experienced seamen refused to sign on for a mysterious trip across unknown waters.

Finally, however, about 250 men agreed to join the expedition. They came mostly from Spain and Portugal, but also included Italians, Frenchmen, Germans, Moors, Africans, and even an Englishman. One of Magellan's most eager recruits was an Italian nobleman, Antonio Pigafetta. The sensitive, well-educated Venetian kept a detailed, daily journal of the voyage,

Magellan and crew set sail aboard their ship,
Victoria, *on a journey around the world.*

one that survives to this day as the most valuable
record of Magellan's adventure.

During his many months of preparation for the voyage, Magellan publicly gave up his Portuguese citizenship and became a citizen of Spain. He also changed the Portuguese spelling of his name and married the beautiful and wealthy Beatriz Barbosa, the daughter of an important Spanish official. Soon he became the father of a son, Rodrigo. Thus the captain-general was not without family on the morning of September 20, 1519, when his five ships prepared to set forth from their Spanish home port.

As cannons boomed and crowds cheered on the dock, Magellan ordered his ships to lift anchor and set sail into the Atlantic. None of those aboard the vessels that day, or among those applauding from the shore beneath the fluttering flags of Spain, possibly could have known how very important, or how very difficult, the voyage would be.

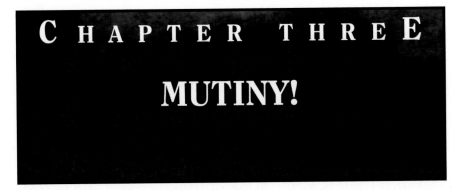

CHAPTER THREE

MUTINY!

Even before Magellan's ships left the harbor, there were problems. King Manuel of Portugal flew into a rage upon learning that his former subject, Magellan, was hoping to find a new trade route to the Spice Islands. The Portuguese first tried to bribe Magellan, offering him money not to make the voyage. When that failed, they tried to damage his ships. There was even a threat to kill him. Those acts only served to toughen Magellan's will. He grew even more eager to discover for Spain a new pathway to Asia.

Not only the Portuguese but also some of the Spanish were plotting against the captain-general. Bishop Juan de Fonseca, who had opposed Columbus's voyage in 1492, was angered by the rich rewards promised to Magellan. The bishop also thought that too many Portuguese sailors had been included in the Spanish fleet.

As a result, Fonseca had Juan de Cartagena, his son and heir, appointed captain of the ship *San Antonio*.

The Bishop of Placentia,
Juan Rodriguez de Fonseca

Two other favorites of Fonseca were made captains of the ships *Victoria* and *Concepción*. As a result, when Magellan's fleet departed from Spain on September 20, 1519, three of his five ships were commanded by men whose loyalty to him was uncertain.

Six days later, on September 26, the vessels landed at the Canary Islands to pick up final supplies. Shortly after they docked, a secret message reached Magellan from his well-placed father-in-law, Diego Barbosa. It warned of a plot to kill the explorer by Cartagena and the other two Portuguese captains chosen by Bishop Fonseca.

Magellan, a tough and experienced military commander, was certain of his ability to handle the situation, but before acting, he would have to wait for the right moment. Leaving the Canary Islands, Magellan surprisingly set a course along the coastline of Africa instead of sailing directly toward South America. Immediately, Juan de Cartagena demanded to know why. Magellan's answer was direct and forceful: "Follow me and ask no questions!" Actually, he had good reason for following the coastal route. Another secret message he had received told him that King Manuel was sending a fleet of Portuguese ships to capture and to kill him.

Magellan's order to his four captains was firm: "Follow my flag by day and my lantern by night." Every evening at sunset he had the four leaders sail close to his flagship, the *Trinidad*, and greet him personally with the traditional naval call: "God save you, Sir Captain-General and Master. . . ." With that simple message, no sailor in the fleet could be uncertain that it was Magellan who was in charge.

The fleet sailed on along the African coastline. Finally, at Sierra Leone, severe storms caused Magellan to sail southwest into the Atlantic. Then the winds died down. Day after day, the blazing hot sun beat down

Magellan plots his navigational course on board the Victoria.

from above. The fleet barely moved in the quiet waters. Soon, the sailors began to grumble and to grow restless.

At last, the winds returned, filling the sails of the ships and sending them speeding across the ocean waves. But still Cartagena was not satisfied. One evening, instead of greeting Magellan himself, he had another officer call out to the captain-general, speaking to him with little respect.

Magellan did nothing at the time. Then, three days later, he asked all four captains to meet with him in the cabin of his ship. Beforehand, he prepared several aides, arming them with swords and guns.

At the meeting Cartagena openly taunted Magellan about the many days the ships had been becalmed at sea. It was Cartagena's plan to provoke the captain-general into a fight and then kill him. When at first Magellan did not answer him, Cartagena saw it as a sign of weakness. Loudly he announced that he no longer would obey Magellan's orders.

That charge was an act of rebellion, exactly what Magellan had been waiting for. At once, he signaled to his men, who entered the cabin with drawn swords. Leaping toward Cartagena, Magellan grabbed him roughly by the shirtfront and forced him into a seat. Refusing to obey orders, declared Magellan firmly, was mutiny! And that, he said, meant that Cartagena should be stripped of his command and be made a prisoner!

Cartagena pleaded with his two friends to plunge

their daggers into Magellan and kill him, but they refused to do so. Magellan ordered the rebel commander thrown into the stocks on deck, as if he were a common criminal.

A few hours later, he released Cartagena, placing him in the custody of two other captains. That evening, Magellan announced to the fleet the appointment of a new captain for the *San Antonio* in place of Cartagena.

Now the days at sea passed quickly under fair winds, good currents, and mild temperatures. At last, in mid-December, Magellan's ships reached the coast of South America. For two weeks, they remained at anchor in the beautiful harbor known today as Rio de Janeiro, Brazil. Magellan's crewmen were treated with great respect by the local people. There were banquets of roasted pigs, as well as fruits that the Europeans never before had tasted. There was card-playing and the trading of goods.

Finally, on the day after Christmas, December 26, 1519, the five Portuguese ships set sail once again. Each day the fleet sailed farther south. But still they found no passageway leading to the western ocean and to the Spice Islands.

Now, south of the equator, in the Southern Hemisphere, they were sailing not into spring and summer but into the colder temperatures of autumn and winter. Storm followed storm. Cold winds, ice, and hailstones pounded away at the wooden vessels. The shoreline revealed nothing but towering gray cliffs and mile after

*By mid-December 1519, Magellan
and his ships had arrived in
Rio de Janeiro, Brazil.*

mile of deserted beachfront. Still, Magellan insisted on
pressing on, searching for a passageway. His sailors,
even his own captains, urged him to return for the winter to the warmer climates of the north. Stubbornly, he
refused even to consider a pause in the journey. At last,
a full-scale mutiny broke out.

The fleet had come to anchor at Port St. Julian, in
the southern area of what is known today as Argentina.

On Palm Sunday 1520, the mutineers, headed by Cartagena, took control of three ships. It was their plan to escape from the harbor and return home immediately to Spain. Magellan, however, managed to send a boatload of his own men, disguised as mutineers, onto

At anchor in Port St. Julian, Argentina

one of the rebel ships. Once aboard, they quickly took control of it and, along with the two ships still loyal to their leader, blockaded the harbor. Using crossbows, lances, and the full broadsides of cannons, Magellan forced the rebellious officers to surrender.

He then called an assembly onshore of all the officers and men of his fleet. In a dramatic trial, one of the mutiny's leaders was found guilty. The captain's own servant, taking great pleasure in the act, cut off the rebel's head. Then, at Magellan's command, the rebel's corpse, along with the body of another mutineer killed in the fighting, were both sliced into quarters, with the insides drawn out and cast into the snow. Pieces of the bodies then were hung from poles overlooking the harbor, for all to see.

At first, Cartagena was spared, but soon afterward he and a priest tried to start another mutiny. Magellan acted firmly. As the fleet set out to sea once again, the explorer left the two men stranded on the lonely shore, pleading on their knees for mercy. Never again would the authority of Ferdinand Magellan be questioned. From that time on, he was the unchallenged master of the Spanish expedition.

CHAPTER FOUR

TRIUMPH

Magellan and his tiny fleet now sailed southward along the coast of South America. As they journeyed onward they saw few signs of human life. There was one exception, though, an encounter with some men of great height who had dry grass wrapped around their feet for warmth. Pigafetta, the Venetian nobleman, described one of them in his journal as a "strange creature, with hair painted white and face daubed with red and yellow." Magellan called the people *Patagones*, meaning "big feet," and ever since, the region has been known as Patagonia.

With the coming of spring, some of Magellan's officers urged him to forget about finding a strait. They argued that the Spanish ships should sail completely around the tip of South America, Cape Horn, and on into the Great "South Sea." Still others simply pleaded that the fleet return to Spain. Meanwhile, one of Magellan's ships, the *Santiago*, was wrecked on a sandbar

Magellan named the people on the southern coast of South America Patagones, *meaning "big feet." The area has since been called Patagonia.*

and had to be abandoned. But Magellan still refused to give up.

At the entrance to one vast bay, he sent two ships ahead to look for a western outlet. Two days passed. On the third day, the ships returned with their cannons booming and flags flying. Nearly 100 miles (160 km) inland, they reported joyously, the water continued to be salty, like that of the sea, as opposed to fresh water, like that of a river. If it was so, this clearly must be the strait! Grateful and humble, Magellan crossed himself and gave thanks to God.

The passageway westward twisted and turned. Countless bays and forks reached into the granite cliffs along its sides. Because of that Magellan sent the *Concepción* and the *San Antonio* to scout along separate routes.

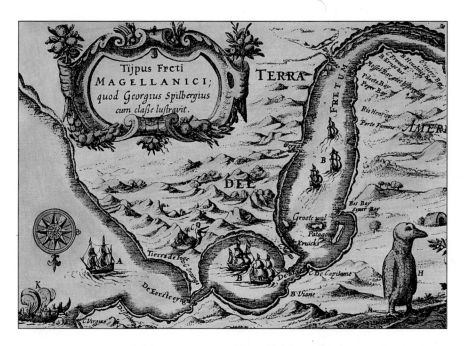

*This map traces Magellan's route
through the strait now named for him.*

After several days, only the *Concepción* returned. The *San Antonio* did not. For three days, Magellan looked for for the missing vessel, the largest ship in his fleet, with the largest reserve supply of food. Finally, he gave up the search and proceeded to the west, suspecting what later turned out to be the truth. The *San Antonio* had deserted, making its way back to Spain. Only three ships now remained in Magellan's fleet.

A few days later, a small boat the captain-general had sent ahead from the *Trinidad* slowly came into view, its crewmen waving their arms and shouting with joy. They had found the outlet to the sea! The silent, controlled Magellan, the man of iron who rarely showed any emotion, gave way to tears.

On November 28, the three remaining Spanish ships sailed out of the channel, known today as the "Strait of Magellan," and into a wide and peaceful ocean. To navigate the stormy, confusing passageway of 375 miles (600 km) had taken more than a month, but Magellan and his men had proved for certain that there was a way through the landmass of the New World.

To celebrate the occasion, all three of Magellan's ships were draped in bunting. In a special ceremony, a priest dressed in formal religious clothing raised a crucifix in thanks and asked the blessing of Our Lady of Victory. The crewmen of the three ships knelt on the decks and sang a *Te Deum*, praising God.

Magellan himself announced that the ships were

Traveling through the stormy strait at the tip of South America was treacherous. The channel today is called the Strait of Magellan, in honor of the first European to successfully sail through it.

now entering into waters where no ship had ever before ventured. Those waters, he prayed, would continue to be as peaceful as they had been that morning. And because they were so tranquil, he would name the sea *"Mar Pacifico,"* the Pacific Ocean. A broadside of cannon then was fired from each of the vessels, ending the ceremony.

For the next three weeks, Magellan sailed northward in the warm sunshine along the coast of what today is known as Chile. Then, with supplies running low, he decided to turn westward into the ocean itself. The maps he was using suggested that the journey westward to Japan, China, and the Spice Islands would be short, only a few days at most. But the ocean was far more vast than Europeans ever had imagined it to be.

Day followed day, with no sight of land. Magellan's three ships already were old when the journey began. After more than fourteen months at sea, the timbers were rotting, the sails patched and mended many times. There was little food to eat, almost no fresh water. Before long, the threat of starvation became real. As Pigafetta described it, the crew "ate biscuit, and when there was none of that, they ate the crumbs, which were full of maggots and smelled strongly of mouse urine. They drank yellow water, already several days putrid."

Desperate, the sailors competed with one another to eat rats they caught in the hold. At last, they even ate odd bits of hide and leather from the ship's fittings. The

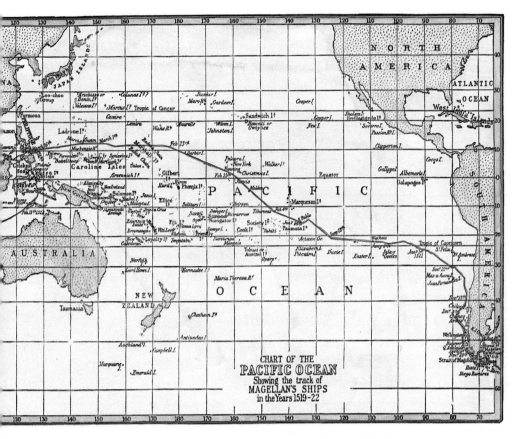

Magellan's route across the Pacific Ocean

world, Magellan now understood, was much larger than his maps had led him to believe. In disgust, he tore the maps into pieces and threw them overboard.

Yet Magellan never lost his courage or his sense of devotion to his men. Each day, he limped from sailor to sailor, trying to offer comfort to them and, as Pigafetta noted, "never once complaining or sinking into despair." By early January 1521, almost a third of the remaining crewmen on the three ships had died.

Finally, at the end of January, the fleet came upon a tiny island. There the sailors rested, fished, and collected rainwater in their canvas sails for drinking purposes. Once again at sea, however, their hunger returned. By March 4, Magellan understood that if they did not find land within the next few days, they all would die. Their food was now completely gone.

Two days later, one of the few sailors still strong enough to climb to the crow's nest shouted with joy, "Land! Land! Praise God! Land!"

It was the island of Guam, but the reception for the three Spanish ships was anything but friendly and gracious. People from the island quickly clambered aboard the vessels, stealing whatever they could. Finally, Magellan ordered his crossbowmen to fire upon them.

When at last the locals fled in fear, Magellan's crewmen rushed ashore. They set fire to the huts they found, and then drank freely from the water supply. They ate bananas, coconuts, rice, chicken and anything else they could find. In the days that followed, they traded with the natives on a nearby island for still more food. Slowly their bodies began to recover.

Once more the ships took to the sea. On March 16, a large island came into view. Then another and another

Magellan realized he had successfully sailed around the world when he heard the Malay language of the people he had visited in 1513.

appeared. Twelve days later, with Magellan's fleet at anchor alongside one of the islands, a canoe carrying eight natives approached the flagship *Trinidad*. It was at this moment that Black Henrique, Magellan's slave, who was standing next to his master at the railing, spoke to the islanders. He addressed them in the Malay language that he had learned as a child on Malacca, on the Malay Peninsula. The natives understood Black Henrique, answering him in Malay! Magellan did not know the words, but he grasped at once what the conversation really meant. He realized that at last he truly had succeeded in circling the globe. He had reached the Philippine Islands, the same cluster of islands he had visited in 1513, while sailing east from Malacca.

At last, it had been established that the world really was round. A ship sailing west from Europe could, indeed, reach the east. Magellan had done what Christopher Columbus had only tried to do and failed. He had reached the Indies.

Now he had only to sail to the Spice Islands, and then return home to his family in Spain with a fortune in gold and spices. According to his contract with King Charles, he then would be entitled to govern the islands he had reached. He would be fabulously rich and forever famous.

But it was not to be.

CHAPTER FIVE

TRAGEDY

The Filipinos were greatly impressed by Magellan's ships. They gazed with admiration at the powerful cannons and other weapons the Europeans so proudly displayed. They were impressed, too, by the Westerner's religion, Christianity. Surely, they must have said, the gods of the Europeans must be very powerful, indeed.

At one ceremony on the island of Cebu, many Filipino chieftains and thousands of their followers knelt in front of a cross. They were then sprinkled with holy water and converted to Christianity. Magellan, a deeply religious man, was enormously pleased. He was happy too when the rajah of Cebu agreed to accept Spanish rule. The rajah said he would become a friend and an ally to his godlike visitors and to their ruler, the Emperor Charles V.

Magellan's officers now urged him to leave at once for the heart of the Spice Islands, but he refused. Grateful to the rajah, and overjoyed with his own successes, he decided to stay to finish one more task. There

*Magellan landed at Cebu
in the Philippine Islands.*

was still one chieftain, the head of the tiny island of
Mactan, who refused to accept Spanish rule. The great
captain-general would not go on with his historic journey until that island, too, had become both Christian
and Spanish. The decision proved fatal.

On April 26, 1521, Magellan personally landed on

 50

Magellan was killed
by an assault of poisoned
arrows and spears.

Mactan with a small force of his own men, but no Filipinos. The next day they were greeted by a flood of arrows, lances, and stones. As his astonished soldiers fled back toward their longboats, Magellan tried to protect their retreat by bringing up the rear. Limping as always from his old wound, he was hit in the leg by a poisoned arrow. Then a spear struck him in the arm, another in the face.

As the loyal Pigafetta later described the scene, "The Indians . . . threw themselves upon him, with spears and scimitars and every weapon they had and ran him through — our mirror, our light, our comforter, our true guide — until they killed him."

Ferdinand Magellan, the "noble captain," was dead.

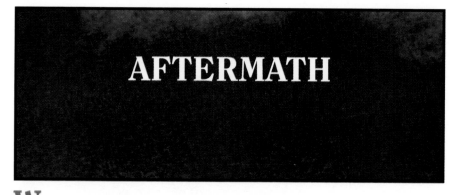

AFTERMATH

With the death of Magellan, the rajah of Cebu and his people no longer considered the Europeans godlike. Before the sailors could escape to the sea, the natives had killed twenty-nine of them. With only 115 men left to man the three ships, it was decided to set fire to the *Concepción*.

In November 1521, the remaining two ships finally reached the Spice Islands. There they found food, as well as gold dust and valuable spices. The *Trinidad,* badly in need of repair, remained behind with fifty-three men, while the *Victoria,* with Juan Sebastian de Elcano in command, set out for Spain.

Seventeen months after Magellan's death, the *Victoria* landed in Seville. Cheering crowds and the roar of naval cannons greeted the ship on its arrival. On board at the time were only eighteen of the men who, nearly three years earlier, had first taken to the sea with Magellan on his voyage. In memory of their beloved captain-general, those men set out, barefooted, and

*Juan Sebastian de Elcano
sailed the* Victoria *back to Seville.*

paraded slowly to Our Lady of Victory, the explorer's favorite church.

As the news of Magellan's voyage began to spread, Europe buzzed with excitement. At last the Earth had

54

truly been proved round, with all the lands surrounded by sea-lanes that ships could navigate. A new age of trade and commerce was about to begin, with the "New World" of the Americas at its very center.

Strangely, Magellan's contribution at first was overlooked. His own carefully kept log had been destroyed, possibly by Elcano, who tried to claim the glory of the voyage for himself. King Manuel of Portugal worked in every way to discredit Magellan, even having the family's noble coat of arms removed from the gate of their estate in Portugal. Meanwhile, even before the Victoria returned home from its great voyage, Magellan's wife, Beatriz, and his young son had both died.

Over the years, however, the great navigator's contribution came to be recognized. Pigafetta made a special effort to restore the captain-general to his proper place in history. To him, Magellan was a man of enormous courage in the face of great difficulty. As Pigafetta wrote:

> He faced hunger more readily than others of us. He was expert in navigation and in the sea charts. . . . No one else had so much natural genius and fortitude, all the knowledge [needed] to circumnavigate the world for the first time, as he did.

Today, nearly five hundred years later, Magellan's greatness is acknowledged, as is his courage. Magellan set

An imaginative artist's interpretation of Magellan's voyage around the world, encountering all sorts of sea animals and monsters

sail in five tiny ships. Since then, our planet has been circumnavigated by machine-powered vessels, and even by submarines. And, in our own time, humankind has embarked on a bold new adventure, the exploration of outer space.

Yet Magellan's journey is seen by many as perhaps the greatest and most wondrous of all ventures in human history. For it was he who overcame plots and treachery at home, as well as mutiny and starvation at sea, to pass through the strait that today bears his name. And from that passageway it was Ferdinand Magellan, too, who, conquering every obstacle, sailed across the mighty Pacific Ocean, changing forever after the way we look at our world.

IMPORTANT DATES

1480	Probable date of Ferdinand Magellan's birth to a noble family in Portugal.
1487	Bartholomew Diaz reaches Cape of Good Hope.
1492	Magellan becomes a page in the court of Leonor, Queen of Portugal.
1492	Columbus discovers America.
1497–1498	Vasco da Gama travels to India.
1505	Magellan accepted as crew member with Portuguese fleet, bound for India.
1507–1515	Magellan serves in Africa, India, and the East Indies. Permanently injured from combat wound while fighting the Moors in Morocco.
1516	King Manuel I of Portugal scorns Magellan's request for increase in pension or for command of a caravel.
1518	King Charles I of Spain (Emperor Charles V) agrees to finance a fleet of five ships under Magellan's command in order to seek a passageway through the Americas to India and the Spice Islands.
1519–September	Magellan's fleet departs from Spain.
1519–December	Fleet arrives at Rio de Janeiro, Brazil.
1520–March-August	Magellan's ships at anchor in Port St. Julian on coast of Argentina.
1520–April 2	Magellan crushes mutiny by commanders of three vessels.
1520–November 28	With only three ships left, the Spanish fleet emerges from "Strait of Magellan" and into sea that Magellan names the "Pacific Ocean."
1521–March 6	Magellan arrives at island of Guam.
1521–March 16	Landing at Cebu in Philippine Islands.
1521–April 27	Magellan killed in battle on Mactan Island.
1522–September 6	The *Victoria*, commanded by de Elcano, arrives in Spain, after circumnavigating the globe.

FOR FURTHER READING

FOR OLDER READERS

Boorstin, Daniel J. *The Discoverers*. New York: Random House, 1983.

Dibner, Bern. *The Victoria and the Triton*. Norwalk, Conn.: Burndy Library, 1962.

Elliott, John Huxtable. *The Old World and the New, 1492–1650*. Cambridge, Mass.: Cambridge University Press, 1970.

Morison, Samuel Eliot. *The European Discoverers of America: The Southern Voyages*. New York: Oxford University Press, 1974.

Parr, Charles McKew. *So Noble a Captain: The Life and Times of Ferdinand Magellan*. New York: Thomas Y. Crowell, 1988.

FOR MIDDLE READERS

Asimov, Isaac. *Ferdinand Magellan*. Milwaukee: Gareth Stevens, Inc., 1991.

Blackwood, Alan. *Ferdinand Magellan*. New York: Franklin Watts, 1986.

Brewster, Scott & Giani Baraldi. *Ferdinand Magellan*, Silver Burdett Press, 1990.

Hargrove, Jim. *Ferdinand Magellan: First Around the World*. Chicago: Childrens Press, 1990.

Humble, Richard & Hook, Richard. *The Voyage of Magellan*. New York: Franklin Watts, 1989.

Lomask, Milton. *Great Lives: Exploration*. New York: Charles Scribner's Sons, 1988.

Stefoff, Rebecca. *Ferdinand Magellan & the Discovery of the World Ocean*. New York: Chelsea House, 1990.

INDEX

Africa, 13, 16, 21, 25, 32
Age of Discovery, 10
Almeida, Francisco de, 16–17

Barbos, Diego, 32
Brazil, 23, 35

Cape Horn, 39
Cape of Good Hope, 13, 25
Cartagena, Juan de, 30–31, 32, 34–35, 37, 38
Cebu, rajah of, 49, 53
Charles V, Holy Roman Emperor (Carlos I, king of Spain), 25–27, 48, 49
Chile, 44
China, 9, 14, 18

Christianity, 10, 49
Columbus, Christopher, 9, 14, 30, 48
Concepcion, 27, 31, 41, 53

Da Gama, Vasco, 13–14
Diaz, Bartholomew, 13, 14

Elcano, Juan Sebastian de, 53, 55

Fonseca, Bishop Juan de, 30–31, 32

Goa, India, 16, 21
Guam, 46

Henrique ("Black Henry"), 19–20, 25, 47–48

Henrique (Henry the
    Navigator), prince of
    Portugal, 13

India, 9, 13–14, 16, 17, 18,
    22

Japan, 14, 18

Leonora, queen of
    Portugal, 14

Mactan, 50–52
Magellan, Beatriz Barbosa,
    29, 55
Magellan, Diogo, 11, 14
Magellan, Ferdinand
    birth and childhood of,
        11, 14
    citizenship changed by,
        28–29
    crews recruited by,
        27–28
    death of, 52
    early voyages of, 14–20
    globe circumnavigated
        by, 10, 48, 54–57
    leg injury of, 20, 21

Malayan slave bought by
    19–20
mutiny against, 36–38
plot against, 30–35
royal patronage sought
    by, 21–23, 25–27
Magellan, Isobel, 11
Magellan, Rodrigo, 29,
    55
Malacca, 18
Malaya, 18
Manuel I, king of Portugal,
    21–23, 25, 30, 32, 55
Miller, Joaquin
    Cincinnatus, 7
Mohammed, sultan of
    Malacca, 18
Mombasa, 16
Moors, 16, 17, 18, 20, 21

North America, 14

Pacific Ocean
    Magellan's voyage
        across, 44–48, 57
    naming of, 44
Patagonia, 39
Philippine Islands, 47–53

Pigafetta, Antonio, 27–28, 39, 44, 46, 52, 55
Portugal, 30, 32
  control over trade routes won by, 16–20
  naval heroes of, 11–14
  wealth of, 21

Sagres, 13
San Antonio, 27, 30–31, 35, 41–42
Serrano, Francisco, 18
Singapore, 16, 18
South America
  Magellan's voyage to, 32–35

search for strait across, 23–24, 35–44, 57
Spain, 14
  Magellan's voyage financed by, 25–27
Spice Islands, 9, 18, 24, 25, 30, 35, 48, 49, 53
Strait of Magellan, 42–44, 57
Straits of Malacca, 9, 18

Trinidad, 27, 32, 42, 47, 53

Venice, 16
Victoria, 27, 31, 53, 55

ABOUT
THE
AUTHOR

William Jay Jacobs has studied history at Harvard, Yale, and Princeton and holds a doctorate from Columbia. He has held fellowships with the Ford Foundation and the National Endowment for the Humanities and served as a Fulbright Fellow in India. In addition to broad teaching experience in public and private secondary schools, he has taught at Rutgers University, at Hunter College, and at Harvard. Dr. Jacobs presently is Visiting Fellow in the Department of History at Yale.

Among his previous books for young readers are biographies of such diverse personalities as Abraham Lincoln, Eleanor Roosevelt, Edgar Allan Poe, Hannibal, Hitler, and Mother Teresa. His *America's Story* and *History of the United States* are among the nation's most widely used textbooks.

In the Franklin Watts First Book series, he is the author of *Magellan, Cortés, Pizarro, La Salle, Champlain,* and *Coronado.*